by Collette Michel
illustrated by Alexandra Colombo

SCHOOL PUBLISHERS

Copyright © by Harcourt, Inc.

All rights reserved. No part of this publication may be reproduced or transmitted in any form or by any means, electronic or mechanical, including photocopy, recording, or any information storage and retrieval system, without permission in writing from the publisher.

Requests for permission to make copies of any part of the work should be addressed to School Permissions and Copyrights, Harcourt, Inc., 6277 Sea Harbor Drive, Orlando, Florida 32887-6777. Fax: 407-345-2418.

HARCOURT and the Harcourt Logo are trademarks of Harcourt, Inc., registered in the United States of America and/or other jurisdictions.

Printed in China

ISBN 10: 0-15-350243-6
ISBN 13: 978-0-15-350243-9

Ordering Options
ISBN 10: 0-15-349030-7 (Grade 4 ELL Collection)
ISBN 13: 978-0-15-349939-5 (Grade 4 ELL Collection)
ISBN 10: 0-15-357291-4 (package of 5)
ISBN 13: 978-0-15-357291-3 (package of 5)

If you have received these materials as examination copies free of charge, Harcourt School Publishers retains title to the materials and they may not be resold. Resale of examination copies is strictly prohibited and is illegal.

Possession of this publication in print format does not entitle users to convert this publication, or any portion of it, into electronic format.

4 5 6 7 8 9 10 985 12 11 10 09 08

Many people have pets. Some people have dogs and cats. Other people have birds. You need to be responsible to have a pet.

Pets need many of the same things people need. Pets need food and shelter. Some pets need to feel like part of a family. Taking care of a pet is a lot of work, but it can be a lot of fun, too!

Sammy and his family have a dog named Buster. There are many different kinds of dogs. Different kinds of dogs are called breeds. A collie is one type of breed. Poodles, spaniels, and terriers are other breeds. Some dogs, like Buster, are a mix of different breeds.

Sammy feeds Buster and gives him fresh water every morning. Then Sammy takes Buster for a walk. Sammy puts a collar around Buster's neck and fastens a leash to the collar.

Scaffolded Language Development

VERB CONJUGATION Remind students that a verb may take a different form depending on the subject. Write the conjugation for the verb *to play* on the board: *I play, you play, he/she plays, we play, they play*. Have students repeat the conjugation of the verb after you several times. Then read each sentence below. Tell students that if the sentence is correct, they should clap their hands. If the sentence is incorrect, they should pat their head. When the sentence is incorrect, invite students to correct it.

1. The dog and the cat plays with each other all the time.
2. My sister and I walks our dog every afternoon.
3. Every morning, I feed my dog and let her out.
4. My family plan to adopt a cat.

Social Studies

Breeds Around the World Explain to students that many breeds of dogs come from different countries. Have students study dog breeds and make a list of various breeds and their countries of origin. Then have students locate each country on a map.

School-Home Connection

Family Pet Ask students to talk with family members about pets they have had or have known. What was involved in caring for the pets?

Word Count: 977

Many different kinds of pets have the same needs. Pets need fresh food and clean water. Many pets need a place to sleep and time for play. A pet needs to go to a doctor if it gets sick.

The most important thing that a pet needs is a person who cares for it. Pets are like friends in some ways. Pets need love and kindness, just like people do!

People also have snakes and lizards as pets. These pets live in glass cases called aquariums. It is important to keep these pets warm, so some aquariums have a light in them. Lizards and snakes eat many different kinds of foods, such as meat, eggs, and insects. Like other pets, it is important to give snakes and lizards fresh water to drink.

Fish also live in an aquarium. The water needs to be kept warm enough for the fish to live. Fish food is sprinkled on top of the water. It is important to keep the water clean, too.

Louie lives in a large cage in Kenji's room. The cage has wood chips in it. Louie likes to dig and burrow in the chips. Each day, Kenji feeds Louie fresh vegetables such as lettuce. Louie also eats a special hamster food that is a mix of different kinds of seeds.

Hamsters need to keep in shape, too. Louie runs in a wheel in his cage. Sometimes Kenji hears Louie running at night. The sound of the spinning wheel lets Kenji know that Louie is a happy hamster.

Every day Carla feeds Chipper birdseed. Chipper also has a special plate inside her cage. The bird pecks on this plate, which keeps her beak from getting too sharp. Carla covers the birdcage with a cloth at night. This cloth helps to keep Chipper warm at night.

Carla's friend Kenji has a very different kind of pet. Kenji's pet is a hamster named Louie. A hamster is a furry animal with whiskers and claws.

Dixie has her own soft and warm bed. Dixie prefers to sleep on Kelly's bed just like Sammy's dog. Even a little cat can take up a lot of room!

Cats and dogs are not the only pets that people have. Kelly's friend Carla has a pet bird. Her little bird talks and sings. Carla keeps her pet bird, Chipper, in a cage. Chipper feels safe and happy in her cage. Carla lets Chipper out of her cage to fly around once a day. This exercise helps to keep Chipper in good shape.

Kelly trims Dixie's claws, too. Trimming her claws keeps Dixie from scratching holes in things.

Cats, like dogs, need exercise to stay in shape. Kelly gives little toys to Dixie. They play every day. Sometimes Dixie even carries her toys over to Kelly so that they can play together!

Many people make sure their pets have identification tags. The pets wear these tags around their necks. Each tag has the pet owner's address and telephone number on it. If a pet gets lost, the person who finds the pet can easily call the owner.

At home, Kelly feeds her cat special cat food. Like dogs, cats need to eat their own food because people food is not good for cats either. Dixie washes herself with her paws after she eats. Cats keep themselves clean. They do not need baths like dogs do.

Kelly brushes Dixie's long fur. Sometimes a cat swallows too much fur when cleaning itself. This causes a hair ball. A hair ball can make a cat sick. Brushing keeps the hairs from getting inside the cat.

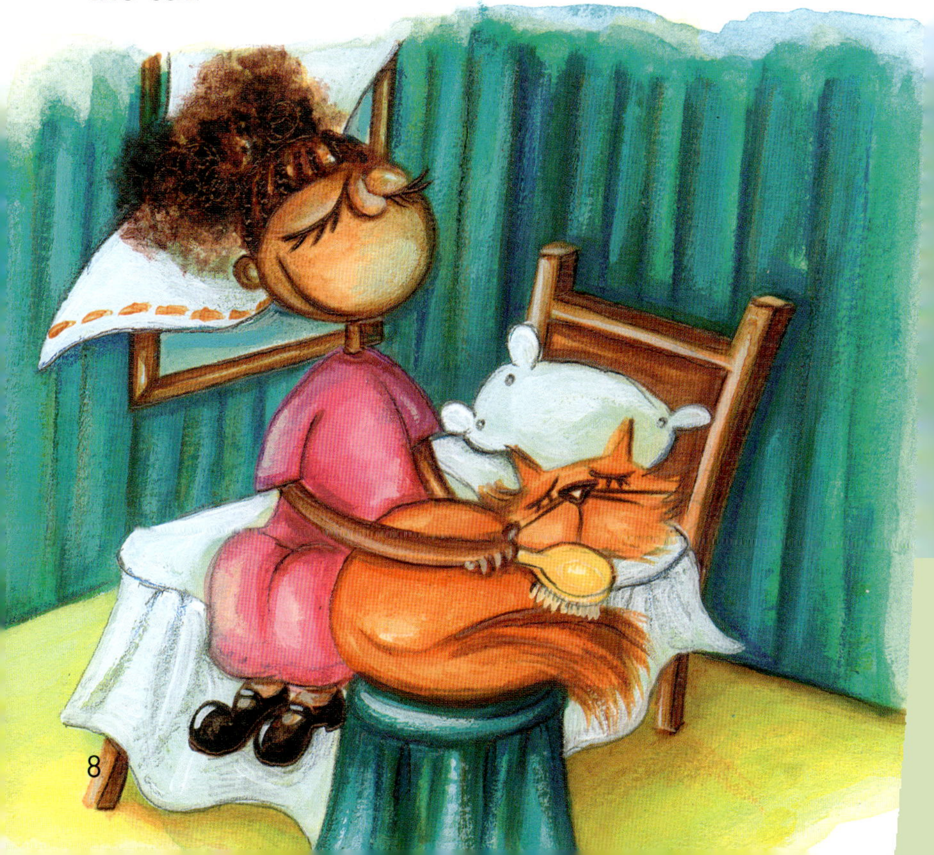

Buster goes to a special doctor for animals called a veterinarian. Buster goes to the animal doctor to get a check-up. The veterinarian checks Buster's heart, and she also looks at his eyes, ears, and teeth. One trip a year to the animal doctor helps to keep Buster healthy.

Other pets are at the veterinarian, too. Kelly takes her cat to the veterinarian. Kelly's cat is named Dixie.

 Sammy feeds Buster his dinner every evening. Buster always eats dog food. People food is not always good for dogs. Foods like bones can hurt dogs because a bone can get stuck in a dog's throat. Sammy gives Buster a chew toy. This toy helps keep Buster's teeth clean. Dogs need healthy teeth just like people do.

 Buster has a special bed to sleep in at night, but Buster likes to sleep on Sammy's bed better. Sometimes Buster takes up the whole bed!

Every day, dogs need to run and play. Sammy throws a ball for Buster to catch. Playing catch is a good way for Buster to get exercise and stay in good shape.

Sammy brushes Buster's fur when Sammy brings Buster inside. Then Sammy checks Buster's paws for sharp objects like thorns. Buster gets a bath once every few weeks. The baths help keep Buster free from ticks and fleas. These are bugs that can bite dogs.